Chapter 1: Introduction to Affiliate Marketing

What is Affiliate Marketing?

Benefits of Affiliate Marketing for Beginners

Chapter 2: Getting Started with Affiliate Marketing

Choosing a Profitable Niche

Finding High-Quality Digital Products to Promote

Selecting a Reliable Affiliate Network

Chapter 3: Building Your Affiliate Marketing Platform

Creating a Professional Website or Blog

Setting Up Social Media Profiles

Building an Email List for Effective Promotions

Chapter 4: Strategies for Successful Affiliate Marketing

Understanding Your Target Audience

Creating Engaging Content to Promote Products

Utilizing SEO Techniques to Drive Traffic

Harnessing the Power of Social Media Marketing

Chapter 5: Maximizing

Your Affiliate Earnings

Implementing Effective Conversion Strategies

Tracking and Analyzing Affiliate Performance

Scaling Your Affiliate Marketing Business

Chapter 6: Avoiding

Common Affiliate Marketing Pitfalls

Recognizing and Avoiding Affiliate Fraud

Dealing with Affiliate Program Terminations

Overcoming Initial Challenges and Setbacks

Chapter 7: Advanced Affiliate Marketing Techniques

Leveraging Influencer Marketing for Affiliate Promotions

Exploring Affiliate Marketing on YouTube

Chapter 8:
Affiliate

Marketing Ethics and Compliance

Understanding FTC Guidelines for Disclosures

Ensuring Transparency and Authenticity in Promotions

Respecting Intellectual Property and Copyright Laws

Chapter 9: Affiliate Marketing Tools and Resources

Essential Affiliate Marketing Tools for Beginners

Recommended Affiliate Marketing Courses and Training

Online Communities and Forums for Affiliate Marketers

Chapter 10: Taking Your Affiliate Marketing to the Next Level

Diversifying Your Affiliate Revenue Streams

Building Long-Term Relationships with Product Creators

Scaling Your Affiliate Marketing Business to New Heights

Chapter 11: Final

Thoughts and Action Steps

Recap of Key Concepts and Strategies

Creating an Action Plan for Affiliate Marketing Success

Embracing a Growth Mindset for Continuous Improvement